Contents

I'm Ali! Look out for our helpful tips throughout the book.

Hi! I'm Annie and this is my dog, Charlie.

Some words are shown in bold, **like this**. You can find out what they mean by looking in the glossary.

Death and grief

You have probably come across death before. You may have read about it in stories or fairy tales. You may have had a pet that has died. Perhaps you have heard about a famous person dying.

When someone you know dies, it feels different. You may have lots of mixed-up feelings. You may feel scared, sad, angry or confused.

Ali and Annie's Guide to...

Coping with
Death and
Grief

Claire Throp

Raintree is an imprint of Capstone Global Library Limited, a company incorporated in England and Wales having its registered office at 264 Banbury Road, Oxford, OX2 7DY – Registered company number: 6695582

www.raintree.co.uk
myorders@raintree.co.uk

Edited by Clare Lewis and Helen Cox Cannons
Designed by Dynamo
Original illustrations © Capstone Global Library Limited 2019
Picture research by Dynamo
Production by Tori Abraham
Originated by Capstone Global Library Limited
Printed and bound in India

ISBN 978 1 4747 7302 7 (hardback)
22 21 20 19 18
10 9 8 7 6 5 4 3 2 1

ISBN 978 1 4747 7308 9 (paperback)
23 22 21 20 19
10 9 8 7 6 5 4 3 2 1

British Library Cataloguing in Publication Data
A full catalogue record for this book is available from the British Library.

Acknowledgements
We would like to thank the following for permission to reproduce photographs:
Getty Images: Blend Images/Inti St Clair, 10, Blend Images/JGI/Jamie Grill, 11, Brand X Pictures/RubberBall Productions, 12, Brand X Pictures/Tetra Images - Rob Lewine, 9, Caiaimage/Tom Merton 26 Right, Cultura/Photo_Concepts, 23, E+/Imgorthand, 7 Bottom Right, E+/Nikada/gradyreese, 18 Middle, E+/Steve Debenport, 24, EyeEm/Monia Severini, 4, iStock/aldomurillo, Cover, 1, iStock/ChesiireCat 22, iStock/GreenAppleNZ, 13, iStock/KatarzynaBialasiewicz, 25, iStock/kzenon 14, iStock/Maica 20, iStock/Nikodash, 16 Bottom Left, iStock/patat, 15, iStock/Wavebreakmedia, 27 Bottom Right, LJM Photo/Design Pics, 17, OJO Images/Paul Bradbury, 28, PhotoAlto/Sigrid Olsson, 5 Middle Right, Photodisc/Rafael Ben-Ari, 19 Bottom Right, Westend61, 6; Shutterstock/Mostovyi Sergii Igorevich, 21.

We would like to thank Charlotte Mitchell for her invaluable help with the preparation of this book.

▲ It can be a big shock when someone you know dies.

What happens when someone dies?

When someone dies, they don't eat, drink or sleep any more. They will no longer feel any pain. You won't be able to see them or talk to them again. They won't ever be alive again. It is difficult to understand why people have to die. But it is something that happens to everyone in the end.

▶ When someone dies, it can seem very final.

You can always remember that person, though. You can think about what they were like whenever you want. You can look at photos or watch videos. Talking to other people who knew them can also help you to remember.

▲ Remembering the good times you had with the person who has died is important.

Why do people die?

TIP

Try to remember that people don't die because of bad things we think, say or do. Don't ever feel it's your fault.

Not everyone dies for the same reason. Most people die when they are old. Others might die from a serious illness. Some people die after being in an accident.

Sometimes we know for a while that a person is going to die. Other times, it can be sudden and a shock to everyone.

▶ Sometimes people are ill for a long time before they die.

Mixed-up feelings

You will probably have lots of feelings at once when you first hear of someone's death. How you work through those feelings is up to you. You might play with your toys, sit quietly or talk to your friends.

TIP

Don't forget, it is OK to feel sad. It is OK to cry. But if you don't feel like crying, that is OK too.

Having strong feelings of sadness when someone dies is called **grieving**. People grieve in different ways. This means that it's hard to give advice about it. Everyone has to find their own way.

Supporting a friend or family member who is grieving is important. But don't pressure them to grieve in a particular way.

Saying goodbye

A **funeral** allows people to say goodbye to the person who has died. Sometimes these **ceremonies** are religious but not always. Loved ones talk about the person's life and how they felt about the person.

After the funeral ceremony, the body of the person who has died is **buried** or **cremated**. When a person is buried they are usually placed in a **coffin**. This can be a plain wooden box or a more colourful one. The coffin is buried in the ground in a grave.

◀ Funerals can be very sad. They can also celebrate a person's life.

It is **traditional** to place flowers on a coffin.

Some bodies are cremated rather than buried. The coffin is placed in an extremely hot room. The body eventually turns to ashes. The ashes are then put in a container called an **urn**.

Some people keep the urn in their home to remind them of their loved one. Others may scatter the ashes in a place that was important to the dead person.

an urn

Visiting your loved one's **grave** is a way of remembering them.

What happens next?

Missing someone who has died is natural. It is especially hard when you do an activity that you used to do with that person. Special times, such as birthdays and Christmas, can also be difficult.

▲ You may feel sad at special occasions.

Spending time with your loved ones can help you deal with your grief.

Talking about it

Talking about feelings can help. Working out what feelings you have may make it easier to ask for help. Are you feeling guilty? Scared? Worried? Sad? Angry? Confused? Lonely?

If you have all of these feelings, that's OK. A person's death is a difficult thing to understand and accept. Putting your feelings into words is hard to do but it can help.

▶ Don't worry about making others feel sad by talking about your own feelings. You do not need to hide your feelings.

TIP

Sometimes, it might feel easier to talk to an adult outside your family. **Counsellors** talk to young people about the problems they may have. Ask your parents or carers if you would like to talk to a counsellor.

▲ **Siblings** can help each other to get through difficult times.

Be creative

Being creative can help you to **express** your feelings. You could keep a diary. Write about your feelings every day or just whenever you feel like it.

You could write a letter or draw a picture for the person who has died. You may want to write down your favourite stories about that person.

You could also make a memory box or scrapbook. Use these to keep photos or **mementos** of the person who has died.

Try making a book to remember the person who has died.

Time helps to heal

It's important to remember that feelings of grief lessen over time. How strong those feelings are can also change from day to day – or even hour to hour.

There is no time limit on grief. Grief can continue for a long time. Eventually, you will feel stronger. It takes a different amount of time for everyone. But healing doesn't mean that you forget the person who has died. You can always remember them with love.

Even after a long time, you may still have sad times.

You do not have to feel sad all of the time. Having fun sometimes is important too.

Understanding death

Everyone dies in the end. If you have questions about death, ask a trusted adult.

Adults may not always have all the answers. They may be able to find out some answers for you. Sometimes just talking about things can still help you to feel better.

TIP

Don't worry about dying. It's important that you have fun in your life. Just remember that most people don't die until they are old.

▲ You may want to talk to a counsellor about your feelings.

Pets

It's not just people we grieve for. The death of a pet can have a huge effect on us. Pets are part of our everyday lives. We see them as part of the family.

TIP

You can remember a pet in the same ways you would remember a person. You can even have a ceremony to say goodbye.

Pets are very important to us.

We spend a lot of time caring for our pets. So when they are gone, it is understandable that we miss them and feel sad.

▲ Like humans, animals can be ill before they die. You may have taken them to see a vet.

Coping with death

It can be very hard to deal with the death of a person you love. But talking about it with your family, friends or even a counsellor can help. Just remember that everyone is different. Nobody should make you feel bad for grieving in the way you do. You know the best way to remember your loved one.

▲ You will have happy times again and you will always remember your loved one.

Ali and Annie's advice

⭐ Remember that people grieve in different ways.

⭐ Talk things through with your friends or family.

⭐ Never feel you are to blame.

⭐ Don't hide your feelings. It doesn't make them go away.

⭐ Ask a trusted adult any questions you have about death.

⭐ Write a letter or draw a picture to help you work things out.

⭐ Remember that it can take time to come to terms with the death of a loved one.

⭐ Make a memory box or photo album of your loved one.

⭐ When you feel ready, celebrate your loved one's life and the time you shared together.

Glossary

buried when a dead person's body is placed underground

ceremony special actions, words or music performed to mark an important event

coffin long, narrow, usually wooden box in which a dead person's body is placed

counsellor person trained to help people suffering from grief or other problems

cremated when the body of a dead person is placed in a very hot room until it turns to ashes

express say or show how you feel to other people

funeral ceremony held after a person's death

grave place where a person is buried

grieve feel extremely sad, sometimes over a long period of time

memento object kept as a reminder of an event or person

sibling brother or sister

traditional beliefs and ways of doing things that have lasted a long time without changing much

urn container that is used to store the ashes of someone who has been cremated

Find out more

Books

What Happened to Daddy's Body?, Elke Barber and
Alex Barber (Jessica Kingsley Publishers, 2016)

When Someone Dies (Questions and Feelings About…),
Dawn Hewitt (Franklin Watts, 2017)

Websites

www.childline.org.uk/info-advice

If you want help about anything, from grief to exams to
families, visit the Childline website.

help2makesense.org/a-z-of-bereavement

This web page has an A–Z of advice about dealing with grief.

Index